FLORIDA STATE
SEMINOLES

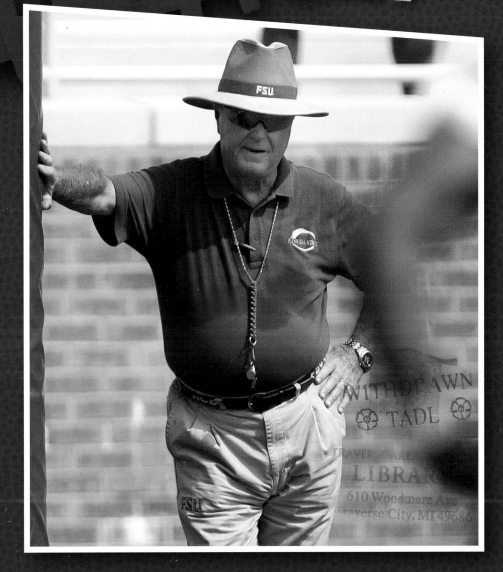

BY ALEX MONNIG

Published by ABDO Publishing Company, PO Box 398166, Minneapolis, MN 55439. Copyright © 2013 by Abdo Consulting Group, Inc. International copyrights reserved in all countries. No part of this book may be reproduced in any form without written permission from the publisher. SportsZone™ is a trademark and logo of ABDO Publishing Company.

Printed in the United States of America,
North Mankato, Minnesota
102012
012013

Editor: Chrös McDougall
Series Designer: Craig Hinton

Photo Credits: Allen Steele/Getty Images, Cover; Phil Coale/AP Images, Title, 37, 43 (bottom, left); Hans Deryk/AP Images, 4, 42 (bottom); Doug Mills/AP Images, 7, 11; Lynne Sladky/AP Images, 9; Tony Strong/Shutterstock Images, 12, 42 (top, left); Gray Quetti/AP Images, 17, 42 (top, right); Collegiate Images/Getty Images, 18, 21; Jim Kerlin/AP Images, 22; AP Images, 24, 31; George Tiedemann/Getty Images, 26, 33; Chris Odom/Getty Images, 28, 43 (top); Mark Foley/AP Images, 34; J. Pat Carter/AP Images, 39; Bob Self/AP Images, 40, 43 (bottom, right); Don Juan Moore/AP Images, 44

Library of Congress Cataloging-in-Publication Data
Monnig, Alex.
 Florida State Seminoles / Alex Monnig.
   p. cm. -- (Inside college football)
Includes bibliographical references and index.
ISBN 978-1-61783-653-4
1. Florida State Seminoles (Football team)--History--Juvenile literature. 2. Florida State University--Football--History--Juvenile literature. I. Title.
796.332--dc15

2012945710

TABLE OF CONTENTS

1 BOWDEN BAGS
THE BIG ONE 5

2 SEMINOLES START LATE 13

3 PETERSON'S PROGRESS 19

4 BOWDEN'S BEGINNINGS 27

5 UPS AND DOWNS 35

TIMELINE 42

QUICK STATS 44

QUOTES & ANECDOTES 45

GLOSSARY 46

FOR MORE INFORMATION 47

INDEX 48

ABOUT THE AUTHOR 48

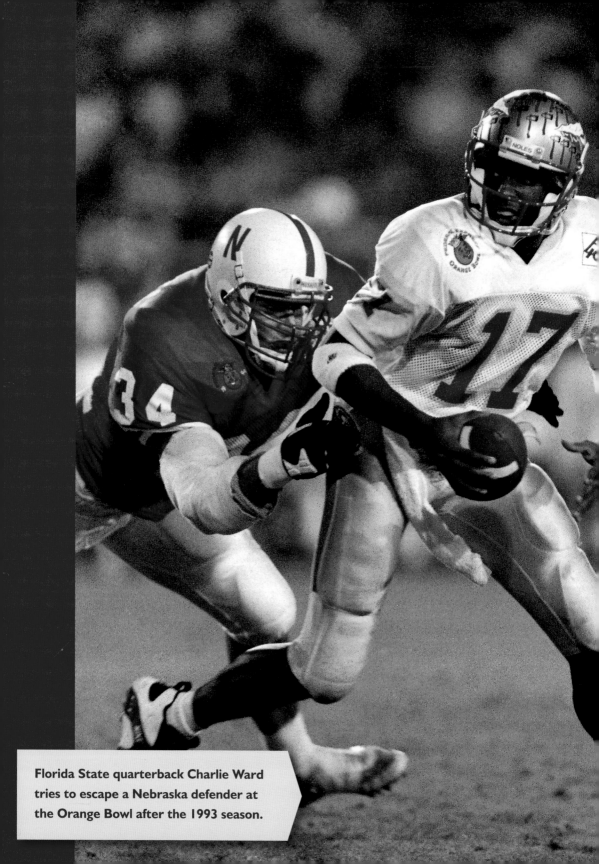

Florida State quarterback Charlie Ward tries to escape a Nebraska defender at the Orange Bowl after the 1993 season.

BOWDEN BAGS THE BIG ONE

IT WAS HAPPENING AGAIN. THE FLORIDA STATE SEMINOLES WERE CLOSE TO WINNING A NATIONAL CHAMPIONSHIP. BUT THE ORANGE BOWL GAME ON JANUARY 1, 1994, AGAINST THE NEBRASKA CORNHUSKERS WAS SLIPPING AWAY.

Coach Bobby Bowden had turned Florida State into a national power since taking over in 1976. Going into the 1993 season, the Seminoles had finished in the top four in the final Associated Press (AP) rankings in each of the previous six seasons. However, the Seminoles had always fallen just short of a national title.

The 1992 squad had come close. Junior quarterback Charlie Ward had been a breakout player in his first season as a full-time starter. He led the Seminoles to a 10–1 record in the regular season. Only one team scored more than Florida State's 37 points per game that season. But even an Orange Bowl victory over Nebraska was not enough. The Seminoles

CHARLIE WARD

Charlie Ward helped make history at Florida State during the 1992 and 1993 seasons. In 1992, he became the first black player to start as the Seminoles' quarterback. As a senior in 1993, he won the school's first Heisman Trophy. Then he led the team to its first national championship.

Ward was known for being both a great runner and a great passer. His talents were not limited to the gridiron, though. Ward also played basketball for Florida State. And he went on to become better known on the hardwood. The New York Knicks selected Ward in the first round of the 1994 National Basketball Association (NBA) Draft. He played 11 seasons in the NBA with the Knicks, the San Antonio Spurs, and the Houston Rockets.

ended the season ranked second in the nation.

Ward, sophomore wide receiver Tamarick Vanover, and other key offensive players returned in 1993. Florida State came into the season ranked first. And it showed why in its first nine games. No team came within 17 points of the Seminoles. Four of those wins had come over ranked teams, one of which was a 28–10 victory over third-ranked Miami.

On November 13, however, Florida State traveled to Notre Dame. It was a rare regular-season game between the country's two top-ranked teams. And the Fighting Irish came out on top 31–24. It appeared that the Seminoles again would fall just short of a national title.

College football is known for its unpredictability, though. Notre Dame lost to Boston College one week later. That reopened the door for Florida State. And with two more wins, the Seminoles ended the regular season back at number one.

Florida State quarterback Charlie Ward tries to make a play during the 1994 Orange Bowl against Nebraska.

Once again the Seminoles were headed to the Orange Bowl. And once again they faced Nebraska. This time, the stakes were even higher. It was only the tenth time the two top-ranked teams had met in a bowl game to that point. That meant the winner would be crowned the national champion.

Both offenses came into the game ranked in the top ten in scoring. Ward had won the Heisman Trophy as the nation's best player. But both offenses got off to a slow start that January 1, 1994, night in Miami, Florida.

BOWDEN BAGS THE BIG ONE

THORN IN THE SIDE

Florida State lost just nine games from 1987 to 1992. Five of those losses came against the Miami Hurricanes. And three of those losses might have cost the Seminoles a shot at the national title. Florida State beat every opponent except Miami in 1987, 1988, and 1992. The Hurricanes went on to win the national title themselves in 1987.

Neither team scored until midway through the second quarter. That is when Florida State freshman kicker Scott Bentley hit a 34-yard field goal to put his team up 3–0. But even a strong effort by Florida State sophomore defensive back Devin Bush could not stop Nebraska from answering soon after. Bush got his hand on a pass. However, Nebraska split end Reggie Baul still was able to catch it for a 34-yard touchdown.

Florida State added another field goal with 29 seconds left in the half. That cut Nebraska's lead to 7–6. But the first half was decidedly defensive. Nebraska sacked Ward four times in the first half alone.

The Seminoles had come into the game as heavy favorites. They started showing why in the second half. Junior running back William Floyd scored a touchdown just a few minutes into the third quarter. Florida State failed to score on a two-point conversion after that. But Bentley hit another field goal in the third quarter. That sent the Seminoles into the final 15 minutes with a 15–7 lead.

Nebraska lost its leading rusher and receiver to injuries in the first half. But despite that setback, the Cornhuskers were soon back in

Florida State wide receiver Kez McCorvey gets tangled up with a Nebraska defender during the 1994 Orange Bowl.

the game. Nebraska running back Lawrence Phillips scored a 12-yard touchdown on the first play of the fourth quarter. After a missed two-point conversion, Florida State's lead was cut to 15–13.

Nebraska quarterback Tommie Frazier led another drive down the field. A 32-yard run by Frazier got the Cornhuskers to the 4-yard line. That set up a successful field goal. With just 1:16 left on the clock, Nebraska now had a 16–15 lead.

BOWDEN'S BOWL BREAK

Bobby Bowden had never won the national championship before the 1993 season. But he was no stranger to success in bowl games. Bowden and the Seminoles were 10–0–1 in bowl games between 1982 and the 1994 Orange Bowl against Nebraska. The lone tie came in the 1984 Citrus Bowl against Georgia. Florida State won two more bowl games to extend the streak to 14. The run was broken when Florida beat the Seminoles 52–20 in the Sugar Bowl following the 1996 season.

Florida State's dreams of a national title appeared to have slipped away. Then came one of the craziest finishes in Orange Bowl history.

Nebraska's kickoff went out of bounds. That gave Florida State the ball on its own 35-yard line. Ward quickly got to work. He led the Seminoles all the way down to Nebraska's 5-yard line. Then, with 21 seconds left, Bentley hit another field goal. Florida State was up 18–16.

The players on Florida State's sideline went crazy. The Seminoles had missed some big field goals in recent seasons. After this successful one, their wild reaction earned them an excessive celebration penalty. That was a sober reminder that the game was not quite over.

The penalty gave Nebraska good field position. And on the second play of the drive, Frazier hit tight end Trumane Bell for a 29-yard pass. But the clock read 0:00. Some Florida State players dumped a cooler out on Bowden in celebration. Others ran out onto the field to celebrate the school's first national title. The public address announcer, however, had an urgent message: "This game is not over!"

The officials ruled that Bell's knee had touched the ground with one second left. So the field was cleared off and the players prepared for one final play. But then the officials came out with another surprise. They decided the spot of the ball was incorrect. So Nebraska's field goal attempt would be from 45 yards instead of 51.

"It seemed like some kind of cruel joke to me," Bowden said. "Really, the crudest joke ever played on me."

Thankfully for Florida State, the joke was soon over. Nebraska's field goal attempt sailed wide left. The Seminoles had finally won a national title. And it would not be their last.

The school existed under many different names before becoming Florida State University in 1947.

SEMINOLES START LATE

FLORIDA STATE UNIVERSITY HAD ITS FIRST STUDENTS IN 1857. IT OFTEN CHANGED NAMES DURING ITS FIRST SEVERAL DECADES. THE SCHOOL WAS LIMITED TO WOMEN FOR LARGE PERIODS AS WELL. BUT FLORIDA GOVERNOR MILLARD CALDWELL CHANGED ALL OF THAT IN 1947. AT THE TIME THE SCHOOL WAS KNOWN AS FLORIDA STATE COLLEGE FOR WOMEN. BUT MANY MALE SOLDIERS WERE RETURNING HOME FROM WORLD WAR II. THUS, CALDWELL RENAMED THE TALLAHASSEE SCHOOL FLORIDA STATE UNIVERSITY AND ALLOWED MEN TO ONCE AGAIN ATTEND.

College football was already well established by that point. The first games had taken place during the late 1800s. So Florida State had a lot of ground to make up.

The school hired Ed Williamson to be the first football coach. He never had much of a chance. Males only arrived on campus a few weeks before the 1947 season. Williamson, a teacher at Florida State, was not even paid for coaching. And the school did not yet have a nickname or logo.

The school soon picked a nickname. The 4,056 students decided to call their teams the Seminoles. The Seminoles were an American Indian tribe in Florida. The tribe had to fight hard to keep settlers from taking its land and changing its traditions. The students wanted that determination and spirit to be reflected in their sports teams.

It took a little longer for the football team to record its first win. The team's first game was a loss against Stetson in October 1947. That was followed by four more losses as the young team ended its first season 0–5. But the losing quickly came to an end.

Florida State became a founding member of the Dixie Conference in 1948. The school hired Don Veller to replace Williamson and lead the way. He had played football at Indiana. Then he had coached at both Indiana and Hanover College. Veller brought much-needed experience to the Florida State program.

His experience showed right away. Florida State went 7–1 in Veller's first season. That included a Dixie Conference title. In fact, Florida State won 30 of its first 34 games under Veller.

Two big reasons for the early success were the play of tackle Hugh Adams and back Buddy Strauss. Adams was the captain of the 1949 team. He was named a Little All-American in 1948 and 1949. That meant he was selected as one of the best players in the country who played at a "little" school.

Strauss was Florida State's first great rusher. He rushed for a combined 1,170 yards in those two seasons. The Seminoles went 8–1 in the 1949 regular season and were invited to the Cigar Bowl. Wofford was favored to win the game. But Strauss was not prepared to lose his final game as a Seminole. He rushed for 132 yards and a touchdown in Florida State's 19–6 victory. His 747 rushing yards that season were a team record until 1972.

Florida State opened Doak S. Campbell Stadium in 1950. It seated just 15,000 fans during its early years. The Seminoles still play there today. However, it is now called Bobby Bowden Field at Doak S. Campbell Stadium. It seats more than 80,000 people.

The Seminoles went 8–0 in 1950, with five of those wins coming at their new stadium. It was their first undefeated season. But things fell

DON VELLER

Don Veller was the first coach to lead Florida State to victory on the football field. He was in charge when the team had its first winning season and when it won its first conference championship. But his contribution to Florida State did not end there. He also spent three different stints as coach of the school's golf team. Veller totaled a 78–23 dual meet record overall as coach. He was so influential in the team's history that Florida State's golf course is named the Don Veller Seminole Golf Course.

SEMINOLES

SEMINOLES SCREEN STARS

Two of the most famous Seminoles to play under Tom Nugent might be better known for what they did on the screen than for what they did on the field. Buddy Reynolds was a freshman on the 1954 squad. He looked like he was going to be a productive pass catcher for the Seminoles before injuries got in the way. However, he later became known as Burt Reynolds and starred in movies and television shows. He was even nominated for an Academy Award in 1998.

Lee Corso played all over the field for Florida State from 1953 to 1956. He led the team in interceptions in 1954, rushing in 1955, and passing in 1956. Then he coached Louisville, Indiana, and Northern Illinois for 15 seasons. Since 1987, Corso has been a host on ESPN's *College GameDay*. It is a popular college football pregame show filmed at a different school each week. Corso picks the winner of the local game by donning the headpiece for that school's mascot.

apart in 1952. The team went just 1–8–1 that season. And Tom Nugent replaced Veller after that.

Nugent was already famous in the college football world. He had invented the I-formation while coaching at Virginia Military Institute. That formation involves the running back lining up behind the fullback, who is lined up behind the quarterback. The setup resembles the letter "I." It is still used in college football today.

Nugent led Florida State to a 34–28–1 record during his six years in charge. The Seminoles went to their second bowl game following the 1954 season. But a poor defensive effort led to a 47–20 loss to Texas Western in the Sun Bowl.

Nugent took the team to another bowl game in 1958. But Florida State again lost. This time, the Seminoles went down 15–6 to Oklahoma State in the Bluegrass Bowl. It was the first time the Seminoles played on national television.

Doak S. Campbell Stadium opened in 1950. Today it seats more than 80,000 people for Seminoles home games.

Nugent did not match Veller's success on the field. But he continued to build a strong foundation for the program. One way he did that was by scheduling tougher opponents. Under Nugent, the Seminoles played proven teams from leagues such as the Southeastern Conference and the Atlantic Coast Conference (ACC). That helped the team improve while also raising the program's profile.

Perhaps the most important game Nugent helped schedule was the 1958 contest against Florida. The Seminoles lost that game 21–7. But the two teams from the Sunshine State would go on to become bitter rivals. And the playing field would get much more even over the years.

[17]

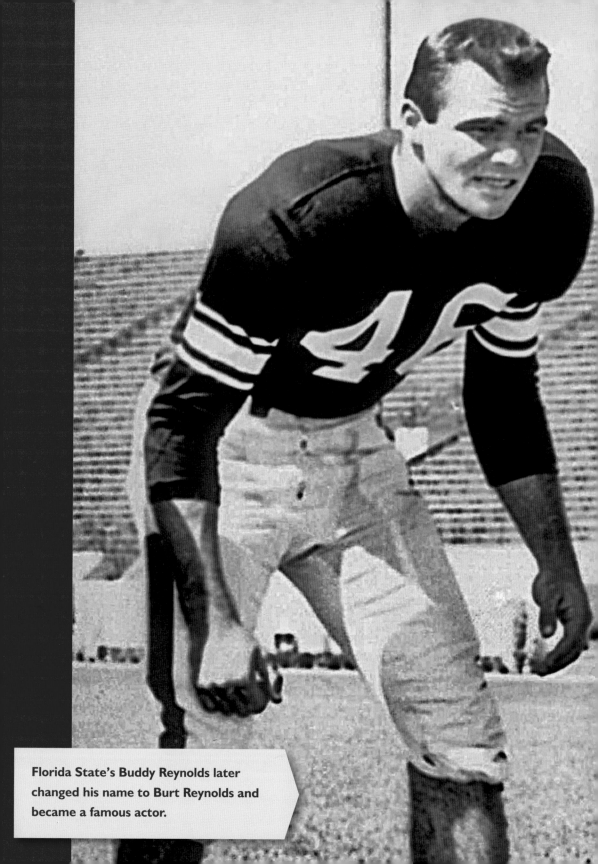

Florida State's Buddy Reynolds later changed his name to Burt Reynolds and became a famous actor.

PETERSON'S PROGRESS

TOM NUGENT HAD BROUGHT SOME LEGITIMACY TO THE FLORIDA STATE PROGRAM. FANS KNEW THE SEMINOLES WERE USUALLY TOUGH TO BEAT. BUT THE TEAM STILL WAS NOT A NATIONAL POWER WHEN NUGENT LEFT FOR MARYLAND AFTER THE 1958 SEASON.

Perry Moss came in after Nugent and coached for one year. The Seminoles finished that season 4–6. Moss left when he was offered $60,000 per year to coach the Montreal Alouettes in the Canadian Football League. That was a huge salary at the time. The school then hired Bill Peterson to continue building a respected team. But the man who came to be known as "Coach Pete" had trouble early.

The Seminoles went just 15–19–6 in Peterson's first four seasons, from 1960 to 1963. A strong offense led a turnaround in 1964. Florida State averaged 24 points per game. That was the ninth best average in the country.

GETTING DEFENSIVE

Bill Peterson became well known for his high-powered offenses at Florida State. But the defense was just as important in the school's breakthrough 1964 season. The Seminoles' tenth-ranked defensive unit allowed fewer than eight points per game. It opened the season with three shutouts. The dominant defensive line was given the nickname of "The Magnificent Seven." It was so good that people often forgot about the quality of the team's defensive backs. That is why they became known as "The Forgotten Four."

One reason for the scoring outburst was wide receiver Fred Biletnikoff. He was one of the best offensive players to ever play college football. In fact, the award given annually to the best college wide receiver is now named the Biletnikoff Award. Biletnikoff played for Florida State from 1962 to 1964. In 1964, he set single-season school records with 57 catches, 987 receiving yards, and 11 touchdowns. For that, he was chosen as Florida State's first consensus All-American.

In 1964, the Seminoles went into their final game with a 7–1–1 record. It was the seventh time Florida State had ever matched up with their in-state rivals, the Florida Gators. And it was the third time the two rivals had met in the regular-season finale. But it was the first time the Gators had come to play the Seminoles in Tallahassee.

The Gators had a message for the Seminoles. Using tape, they wrote on the side of their helmets: "Never FSU, Never." A plane even flew over the stadium with a banner that said "Never." That was because the Seminoles had never beaten the Gators.

That finally changed on that day in 1964. Florida State jumped out to a 7–0 lead over Florida after a 55-yard touchdown catch by Biletnikoff. Meanwhile, Florida State's defense forced six turnovers. That helped Florida State record the 16–7 win. The victory also sent the Seminoles to the Gator Bowl.

Florida State star wide receiver Fred Biletnikoff makes a catch while practicing for the Gator Bowl after the 1964 season.

"It put us on the map," quarterback Steve Tensi said of the win.

The Seminoles faced the Oklahoma Sooners in the Gator Bowl. Biletnikoff was unstoppable in the game. He caught 13 passes for 192 yards and four touchdowns. The Seminoles beat Oklahoma 36–19 to finish the season 9–1–1.

"Well, I wish it was the coaching, but he was a natural," Bobby Bowden, then wide receivers coach, said of Biletnikoff. "When I came down here, I coached the wide receivers. He was a defensive back, but he could really catch the ball. Our offensive coordinator, Bill Crutchfield, made a receiver out of him and he was just a natural."

With Biletnikoff gone to professional football, Florida State leveled out to 4–5–1 in 1965. Then Peterson led the Seminoles to five straight winning seasons from 1966 to 1970. Again Peterson's explosive offense led the way. And a new star wide receiver took center stage.

Ron Sellers played for Florida State from 1966 to 1968. During that time, he set career records with 212 catches and 3,598 receiving yards. Those marks stood at Florida State for decades.

The Seminoles played in three bowl games over that stretch from 1966 to 1968. But they were not able to

PETERSON'S PROTÉGÉS

Bill Peterson was one of the driving forces behind Florida State's improvement in the 1960s. He also was the driving force behind the growth of several coaches who would become legends in the game. Peterson had a knack for finding talented young coaches and hiring them as assistants. Two of them were Bill Parcells and Joe Gibbs. Both went on to have successful careers in the National Football League (NFL).

Parcells won two Super Bowls with the New York Giants. He also coached the New England Patriots, the New York Jets, and the Dallas Cowboys. Gibbs won three Super Bowls with the Washington Redskins. But Peterson's most well-known assistant, at least in Tallahassee, was Bobby Bowden. He went on to win a Division I record 346 games, including 304 at Florida State. Bowden also coached the Seminoles to two national titles.

PETERSON'S PROGRESS

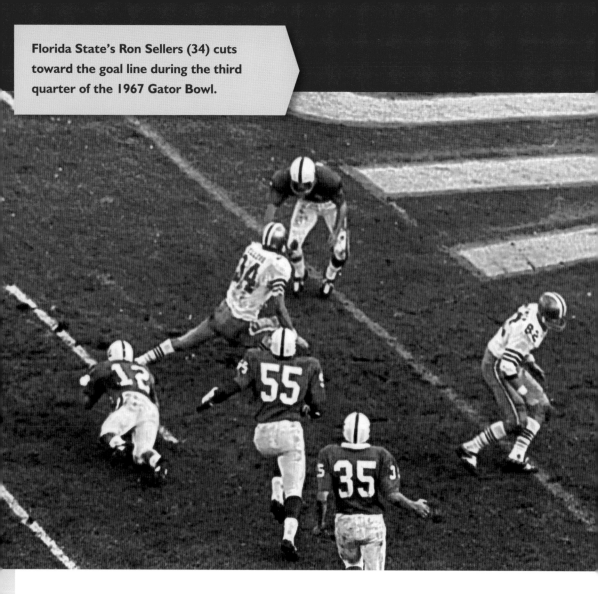

recapture their form from the Gator Bowl played after the 1964 season. Florida State lost to Wyoming in the 1966 Sun Bowl. It tied Penn State in the Gator Bowl in 1967. And it lost to Louisiana State University in the 1968 Peach Bowl.

Peterson left the school after the 1970 season to coach at Rice. Larry Jones replaced him. Jones continued what Peterson had started by going 15–8 over the 1971 and 1972 seasons. But then things went downhill.

HE SAID IT

"I really think that if I had stayed at Florida State, I still might be there today, because they were just on the verge of becoming a power. I regret leaving there." —Former Florida State coach Perry Moss, who coached the Seminoles in 1959, in 1987

Some players said Jones forced them to attend an offseason class for training. While there they said they were required to wrestle each other beneath barbed wire. Ultimately, 28 of them ended up quitting the team.

The next season was one of the worst in team history. Florida State went 0–11. Jones was fired after that. But things did not get much better under new coach Darrell Mudra. He lasted only two seasons. The Seminoles were a pitiful 4–18 during that time. Much of the good work Peterson had accomplished was being undone by scandal and poor performances on the field. But it was not long before Florida State fans were again given a reason to cheer.

Bobby Bowden coached Florida State to
304 wins and two national titles between
1976 and 2009.

4

BOWDEN'S BEGINNINGS

BOBBY BOWDEN TOOK OVER AT A TROUBLING TIME IN FLORIDA STATE HISTORY. THE PREVIOUS THREE SEASONS HAD BEEN A MESS. THE TEAM HAD BEEN ACCUSED OF SCANDAL. AND ITS RECORD IN THOSE SEASONS WAS A MISERABLE 4–29. THE SEMINOLES, WHO HAD MADE SO MUCH PROGRESS, WERE IN DANGER OF AGAIN BECOMING A LAUGHINGSTOCK.

Bowden had been an assistant under Bill Peterson. He had left Florida State to become an assistant coach at West Virginia. After taking over as West Virginia's head coach in 1970, he had five winning seasons in six years there. Bowden then returned to Tallahassee in 1976 to try to save the struggling Seminoles.

Florida State went 5–6 in Bowden's first year as head coach. That was more wins than in the three previous seasons combined. Then the team jumped to 10–2 in 1977. It was the first time a major college football team from Florida had won 10 games in a season. The Seminoles also beat the

Florida Gators for the first time in 10 years. That started a string of four straight victories over their rivals from Gainesville. Florida State ended the season with a 40–17 win over Texas Tech in the Tangerine Bowl. It was the team's first bowl victory since the 1964 season.

The Seminoles were nearly perfect in 1979. Senior quarterbacks Jimmy Jordan and Wally Woodham led the offense. All-American junior tackle Ron Simmons led the defense. Florida State started the season 11–0. It climbed all the way up to number four in the AP Poll. That earned the Seminoles a trip to the Orange Bowl to face Oklahoma.

National champions at the time were determined by polls, such as the AP Poll. The Seminoles went into the Orange Bowl undefeated. However, their national championship hopes were slim. Three other teams were also undefeated and ranked higher than Florida State. All three would likely have to lose their bowl games for Florida State to claim the title.

None of that ended up mattering. Oklahoma beat Florida State 24–7. But the Seminoles still finished the season ranked sixth in the AP Poll. It was their highest end-of-season ranking to that point.

Much of the team's talented defense returned in 1980. Three All-Americans, Simmons and senior defensive backs Monk Bonasorte and Bobby Butler, led a shutdown defense. Only one team allowed fewer points per game than Florida State.

The Seminoles finished the regular season 10–1. This time, they had beaten third-ranked Nebraska and fourth-ranked Pittsburgh along the

CHIEF OSCEOLA AND RENEGADE

In 1962, Florida State sophomore Bill Durham came up with an idea. He wanted a person dressed and painted as a native Seminole Indian to ride into the stadium on a horse and plant a spear at midfield before each game. The concept did not get much attention until Bowden took over as coach. He liked it. Chief Osceola and his horse Renegade debuted in 1978. They rode to the middle of the field and jammed a spear into the turf before kickoff of a game against Oklahoma State. The Seminoles went on to win 38–20. The tradition still exists today.

way. So they came into the Orange Bowl ranked second in the nation. Only the Georgia Bulldogs were ranked higher. The Seminoles faced fourth-ranked Oklahoma in the Orange Bowl. A win plus a Georgia loss could have meant a national title.

Florida State was ahead 17–10 with less than two minutes to go. But Oklahoma scored a touchdown and a two-point conversion to win 18–17. So Florida State ended the season ranked fifth in the AP Poll.

Bowden had brought the Gators to the top of college football within his first five seasons. The next six years were not quite as strong. Florida State was 45–23–3 from 1981 to 1986. Those numbers were not bad. But after the highs of 1979 and 1980, the record seemed mediocre.

The spectacular seasons soon returned. In 1987, Florida State started a streak in which it finished among the top five of the AP Poll 14 years in a row. The Seminoles were 152–19–1 from 1987 to 2000. The offense ranked in the top ten in scoring 13 times during that span.

NEON DEION

Deion Sanders set a new standard for cornerbacks. From 1985 to 1988, he had 14 interceptions—four of them for touchdowns—for Florida State. He also ran back a school-record 1,429 yards on punts. That helped him win the 1988 Jim Thorpe Award as college football's best defensive back. Sanders was also known for his flair. His exciting play and flashy style earned him the nicknames "Neon Deion" and "Prime Time." Sanders went on to play both in the NFL and in Major League Baseball. He is enshrined in the pro and college football halls of fame.

Florida State cornerback Deion Sanders reacts after the Atlanta Falcons selected him in the 1989 NFL Draft.

Two Florida schools defined the 1987 season. The Seminoles and the Miami Hurricanes were developing a fierce rivalry. Both were ranked among the top four when they met in the fifth game that season.

The Seminoles started strong. But then Miami came back to take the lead. A late touchdown brought the Seminoles to within one point. They could have tied the game with an extra point. Instead, Bowden went for the two-point conversion. Miami's defense held, sealing a 26–25 win. It ended up being the crucial result in the national title picture that year.

Neither team lost the rest of the season. Miami went on to win the national championship. Florida State, meanwhile, finished second in the AP Poll after beating Nebraska in the Fiesta Bowl.

BOWDEN'S BEGINNINGS

FOILED BY FLORIDA

The Seminoles had plenty of trouble with Miami during the late 1980s and throughout the 1990s. But they enjoyed plenty of success against Florida. Florida State had an 11–4–1 record against the Gators from 1987 to 2000.

Florida came to Tallahassee in 1996 as the top-ranked team in the AP Poll. Florida State was ranked second. The Seminoles pressured Florida's Heisman Trophy-winning quarterback Danny Wuerffel. It helped them upset the Gators 24–21. Florida State went on to finish the regular season 11–0.

However, they again met in that season's Sugar Bowl. This time, Florida State was ranked first and Florida was ranked third. If the Seminoles won, they would likely be national champions. But Florida State would have to wait for its second title. Wuerffel threw for three touchdowns as the Gators won 52–20 and took the national title.

The 1988 season had a similar story. Florida State came into the season ranked first in the AP Poll. But sixth-ranked Miami was waiting in the season opener. This time it was not even close. The Hurricanes rolled over the Seminoles 31–0. And once again, the Seminoles did not lose another game. They finished the season ranked third.

The Seminoles had become a premier team under Bowden. So on March 30, 1990, he signed a "lifetime" contract to be the school's football coach. That meant he could continue to coach for as long as he wanted.

Bowden soon had the Seminoles back in the national-title picture. They won their first 10 games of the 1991 season. Then the top-ranked Seminoles faced the second-ranked Hurricanes in Tallahassee. Miami led 17–16 with 25 seconds to go. But Florida State was in field-goal range with a chance to win. Instead, sophomore kicker Gerry Thomas watched his 34-yard attempt

sail wide right. A loss to Florida the next week dropped the Seminoles out of contention.

A similar story played out in 1992. Miami was ranked second and Florida State third when they met on October 3. And it was again a tight game. Florida State sophomore kicker Dan Mowrey attempted a 39-yard field goal to tie the game. But just as it had the season before, it sailed wide right. The 19–16 loss was Florida State's only one that season. The Seminoles finished the year ranked second.

Finally, just when it seemed like an important field goal would never go Florida State's way, one did. When Nebraska missed a game-ending field goal in the Orange Bowl following the 1993 season, Bowden and Florida State had finally done it. They were national champions at last.

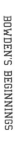

BOWDEN'S BEGINNINGS

Florida State running back Warrick Dunn moves the ball against Virginia during a 1996 game.

5

UPS AND DOWNS

THE JOY OF FLORIDA STATE'S 1993 NATIONAL TITLE WAS A LONG TIME COMING. BUT THE VICTORY WAS SOON PARTIALLY OVERSHADOWED BY CONTROVERSY.

The National Collegiate Athletic Association (NCAA) has strict rules for its athletes. Among them is that athletes are not allowed to accept gifts or money while playing sports. Some Florida State players nearly broke those rules. Agents reportedly paid the players so that the players would sign with them for representation after college.

The Seminoles escaped the accusations without punishment. And they continued winning. Sophomore running back Warrick Dunn led Florida State in 1994. The Seminoles had the fifth-ranked offense at just under 36 points per game. But Florida State's dreams of repeating as champions were dashed by two familiar foes. The Seminoles lost to Miami and tied Florida in the regular season.

SEMINOLES

CHRIS WEINKE

Quarterback Chris Weinke attempted just 13 passes as a freshman in 1997. Then he took over as starter in 1998. It was rare for coach Bobby Bowden to let a sophomore start at quarterback. But at 25, Weinke was older than most sophomores after a minor league baseball career. He led the Seminoles to just under 31 points per game that year. That ranked twenty-ninth in the country. While still good, it was low for the Seminoles.

Soon the Seminoles were back to their high-powered ways. Weinke threw for 3,432 yards and 29 touchdowns in 1999. Florida State scored more than 38 points per game that year. Most importantly, the team had its first undefeated season and won its second national championship. Weinke saved his best personal season for last. As a senior in 2000, he threw for 4,167 yards and 33 touchdowns. That was good enough to earn him the Heisman Trophy.

Florida State was back in the national title hunt in 1996 and 1997. But the Gators kept the Seminoles from getting back to the very top. In 1996, Bowden's squad was undefeated in the regular season. That included a win over Florida. But the Seminoles and the Gators again faced off in that year's Sugar Bowl. In the rematch, Florida crushed Florida State's dreams of a second national title with a 52–20 win.

The Gators remained an obstacle. Florida State was 10–0 and ranked second heading into its game with Florida in 1997. A win would have given the Seminoles a shot at another national title. But the Gators once again downed Florida State, this time 32–29.

The Seminoles came into the 1998 season ranked second in the AP Poll. They lost to unranked North Carolina State in their second game. But they climbed back to number two. No team came within eleven points of the Seminoles the rest of the season.

That is, until they met top-ranked Tennessee in the Fiesta Bowl. The Seminoles lost 23–16. They had again come within one win of a potential national championship.

Sophomore quarterback Chris Weinke had taken over as the starter that season. He had shown some potential then. And he only improved in 1999. The Seminoles came into the season ranked first in the AP Poll. They stayed there the whole year.

Undefeated Florida State met Virginia Tech in the Sugar Bowl. Florida State had been ranked number one all season. Virginia Tech,

UPS AND DOWNS

meanwhile, was ranked second. That meant the winner would be named the national champion.

Florida State left no questions about its number one ranking. The Seminoles dominated in a 46–29 rout. Weinke threw for 329 yards and four touchdowns. After several close calls, the Seminoles had finally captured their second title. The 12–0 finish represented the first time Florida State had finished a season undefeated.

History looked like it might repeat itself in a few different ways in 2000. The top-ranked Seminoles entered their matchup with seventh-ranked Miami 5–0. Just like in 1991 and 1992, the game came down to a late Seminoles field-goal attempt. This time, freshman kicker Matt Munyon missed from 49 yards on the final play. Another kick sailing wide right against Miami looked like it cost Florida State a chance at the title.

But the Seminoles fought back. The Bowl Championship Series (BCS) was created in 1998 to pit the top teams against each other in the biggest bowl games. Some were surprised when the BCS formula had Florida State in the Orange Bowl. Nonetheless on January 3, 2001, the Seminoles played Oklahoma for the national title. However, the Sooners defense smothered Weinke. The Seminoles lost 13–2.

Since 1987, Florida State had finished each season ranked among the AP Poll's top five. That streak finally ended in 2001. The 8–4 Seminoles finished fifteenth. From 2002 to 2005, the Seminoles went 36–16. The wins were still coming. But they were not at the rate that fans of the program were used to.

In the spring of 2007, Bowden learned he had prostate cancer. He kept the news to himself. He did not want his health problems to get in the way of Florida State's recruiting. But the team finished a disappointing 7–6 that season.

The program took another blow before the Music City Bowl that year against Kentucky. It was discovered that the NCAA was investigating 25 Florida State players for various academic issues, including cheating on schoolwork. The NCAA ended up suspending them for the bowl game. But the punishments did not stop there. Florida State also had to give up 12 wins in which those players had participated.

Florida State bounced back from the scandal to go 9–4 in 2008. But the Seminoles fell back to 7–6 in 2009. By then, Bowden was 80 years

UPS AND DOWNS

old. He announced that the team's Gator Bowl appearance that year would be his last as head coach. Florida State sent him out on a winning note by beating West Virginia—the school where he had gotten his first head coaching job. He finished his career with 377 wins.

Offensive coordinator Jimbo Fisher had been named Florida State's coach-in-waiting in 2007. Some Florida State fans were upset with Bowden's exit. They felt the coach had been forced out of his job. Either way, Fisher took over as planned in 2010. The new coach had a tough act to follow. Bowden was one of the most successful head coaches in

ROLLE THE RHODES SCHOLAR

Florida State was getting negative attention for off-field reasons toward the end of Bobby Bowden's time as head coach. But safety Myron Rolle was not to blame. In November 2008 he was awarded a Rhodes scholarship. The scholarship winners are able to go study at the famous Oxford University in England. Rolle had a tough decision to make. Many said he was good enough to get selected early in the NFL Draft. But Rolle decided to skip his senior football season to attend Oxford. He was later selected in the sixth round of the 2010 NFL Draft.

college football history. But the Seminoles got off to a 10–4 start under Fisher in 2010. It was their first 10-win season since 2003. He followed up that with a 9–4 season in 2011.

It appeared Fisher had the Seminoles back on track for another generation of greatness.

TIMELINE

Governor Millard Caldwell signs a bill to make the Florida State College for Women co-educational. Florida State University is born.

In October, Florida State plays its first football game, which is a loss to Stetson.

On January 2, Florida State defeats Wofford 19–6 in the Seminoles' first bowl game.

Florida State builds Doak S. Campbell Stadium. It holds 15,000 fans at the time.

Florida State plays Florida for the first time on November 22. The Seminoles go down 21–7.

1947   1947   1950   1950   1958

On November 16, Seminoles sophomore kicker Gerry Thomas misses a field goal in the final minute of a 17–16 loss to Miami. It is the first of several crucial missed kicks for Florida State.

Florida State joins the ACC and wins the first of its many conference championships.

Senior quarterback Charlie Ward becomes the first Seminole to win the Heisman Trophy.

On January 1, Florida State defeats Nebraska 18–16 in the Orange Bowl to win the Seminoles' first national championship.

Florida State players are accused of accepting improper gifts during the 1993 season.

1991   1992   1993   1994   1994

On November 21, the Seminoles beat Florida 16–7 for their first win over the Gators.

Bobby Bowden leads the Seminoles in his first game as Florida State's head coach. The team loses 21–12 to Memphis State on September 11.

Florida State becomes the first major college football team from Florida to win 10 games in a season.

A Florida State tradition begins when a person dressed as Chief Osceola rides out on a horse named Renegade before the home opener on September 16.

Bowden signs a "lifetime" contract with Florida State on March 30.

1964 1976 1977 1978 1990

The team's first undefeated season culminates on January 4, as Florida State routs Virginia Tech 46–29 in the Sugar Bowl to win the school's second national championship.

Senior quarterback Chris Weinke becomes the second Seminole to win the Heisman Trophy.

In a ceremony before a game against Florida on November 20, the turf at Doak S. Campbell Stadium is named Bobby Bowden Field.

Bowden is diagnosed with prostate cancer. A cheating scandal forces 25 players to be suspended.

Bowden coaches his final game. The Seminoles send him out on a winning note by defeating West Virginia 33–21 in the Gator Bowl on January 1.

2000 2000 2004 2007 2010

QUICK STATS

PROGRAM INFO
Florida State University Seminoles (1947–)

NATIONAL CHAMPIONSHIPS
1993, 1999

OTHER ACHIEVEMENTS
BCS bowl appearances (1999–): 5
ACC championships: (1992–): 12
Bowl record: 24–14–2

HEISMAN TROPHY WINNERS
Charlie Ward, 1993
Chris Weinke, 2000

KEY PLAYERS
[POSITION[S]; SEASONS WITH TEAM]
Fred Biletnikoff (WR; 1962–64)
Monk Bonasorte (DB; 1977–80)
Bobby Butler (DB; 1977–80)
Lee Corso (QB/CB; 1953–56)
Jimmy Jordan (QB; 1976–79)
Ron Sellers (WR; 1966–68)
Ron Simmons (G; 1977–80)
Buddy Strauss (B; 1948–49)
Tamarick Vanover (WR; 1992–93)

Charlie Ward (QB; 1989, 1991–93)
Chris Weinke (QB; 1997–2000)
Wally Woodham (QB; 1977–79)

KEY COACHES
Bobby Bowden (1976–2009):
    304–97–4; 21–9–1 (bowl games)
Bill Peterson (1960–70):
    62–42–11; 1–2–1 (bowl games)

HOME STADIUM
Bobby Bowden Field at
    Doak S. Campbell Stadium (1950–)

* All statistics through 2011 season

"The fact is, when I came to Florida State, we had no male alumni over 40. Since Tallahassee was a small city of about 50,000, few alumni were still in the city. The school was independent and therefore had neither a winning tradition nor an identification with a conference." —Seminoles coach Bill Peterson, explaining some of the difficulties and lack of support facing him when he arrived in 1960

Florida State has a section of its practice field called the Sod Cemetery. At a 1962 practice, a Florida State teacher and member of the school's athletic board challenged the team to win its game at Georgia and bring back a piece of sod from the field. The team won, so captain Gene McDowell brought a chunk of grass back to Tallahassee. It was buried outside the gates of the practice field. Now, any time Florida State is an underdog, plays at Florida, plays in an ACC Championship Game, or plays a bowl game, the players bring back a piece of their opponent's field to add to the Sod Cemetery.

Three of Bobby Bowden's sons also have patrolled the sidelines at major colleges. Terry Bowden coached at Auburn from 1993 to 1998 where he led his team to an undefeated season in his first year. He was hired at Akron in 2012. Tommy Bowden coached at Tulane from 1997 to 1998, leading his team to an undefeated season in his second year. He then coached at Clemson from 1999 to 2008. And Jeff Bowden has been an assistant coach at several schools.

GLOSSARY

agent
A person who handles a professional player's business dealings.

All-American
A player chosen as one of the best amateurs in the country in a particular activity.

conference
In sports, a group of teams that play each other each season.

consensus
Unanimous agreement.

contract
An agreement between a team and a coach that determines the coach's salary and length of commitment with that team.

draft
A system used by professional sports leagues to select new players in order to spread incoming talent among all teams. The NFL Draft is held each April.

mediocre
Not good but not bad.

recruiting
Trying to entice a player to come to a certain school.

rivals
Opponents that bring out great emotion in the other team's players and fans.

scandal
A disgraceful incident.

scholarship
Financial assistance awarded to a student to help them pay for school.

upset
A game in which the team expected to lose ends up winning.

FOR MORE INFORMATION

FURTHER READING

Fleder, Rob. *Sports Illustrated: The College Football Book*. New York: Sports Illustrated Books, 2008.

Hinds, John. *Florida State University Football Vault*. Atlanta, GA: Whitman Publishing, 2008.

Schlabach, Mark. *What it Means to Be a Seminole: Bobby Bowden and Florida State's Greatest Players*. Chicago, IL: Triumph Books, 2007.

WEB LINKS

To learn more about the Florida State Seminoles, visit ABDO Publishing Company online at **www.abdopublishing.com**. Web sites about the Seminoles are featured on our Book Links page. These links are routinely monitored and updated to provide the most current information available.

PLACES TO VISIT

**Bobby Bowden Field at
Doak S. Campbell Stadium**
403 Stadium Drive West
Tallahassee, FL 32306
850-644-6710
**www.seminoles.com/facilities/fsu-trads-
fac-campbell.html**

This has been Florida State's home stadium since 1950. Tours are available seven days a week.

College Football Hall of Fame
111 South St. Joseph St.
South Bend, IN 46601
1-800-440-FAME (3263)
www.collegefootball.org

This hall of fame and museum highlights the greatest players and moments in the history of college football. Among the former Seminoles enshrined here are Charlie Ward and Bobby Bowden.

Florida Sports Hall of Fame
905 Lake Myrtle Park Drive
Auburndale, Florida 33823
863-551-4750
www.floridasportshalloffame.com

This is hall of fame and museum features tributes to famous athletes and coaches in Florida sports history.

INDEX

Adams, Hugh, 14–15

Baul, Reggie, 8

Bentley, Scott, 8, 10

Biletnikoff, Fred, 20, 21, 22, 23

Bonasorte, Monk, 29

Bowden, Bobby (coach), 5, 10–11, 15, 23, 27, 29, 30–33, 36, 39–41

Bush, Devin, 8

Butler, Bobby, 29

Chief Osceola, 29

Corso, Lee, 16

Crutchfield, Bill (offensive coordinator), 23

Doak S. Campbell Stadium, 15

Dunn, Warrick, 35

Fiesta Bowl, 31, 37

Fisher, Jimbo (coach), 40, 41

Florida, 17, 20–21, 28, 32–33, 35–36

Floyd, William, 8

Gator Bowl, 21, 22, 24, 40

Jones, Larry (coach), 24–25

Jordan, Jimmy, 28

Miami, 6, 7, 8, 31–33, 35, 38

Moss, Perry (coach), 19, 25

Mowrey, Dan, 33

Mudra, Darrell, 25

Munyon, Matt, 38

Nebraska, 5–11, 29, 31, 33

Nugent, Tom (coach), 16, 17, 19

Oklahoma, 22, 28–29, 30, 38

Orange Bowl, 5, 7, 10, 28–30, 33, 38

Peterson, Bill (coach), 19, 20, 23–24, 27

Reynolds, Buddy (Burt), 16

Rolle, Myron, 41

Sanders, Deion, 30

Sellers, Rob, 23

Simmons, Ron, 28–29

Strauss, Buddy, 14–15

Sugar Bowl, 10, 32, 36–37

Tensi, Steve, 22

Thomas, Gerry, 32

Vanover, Tamarick, 6,

Veller, Don (coach), 14–15, 16, 17

Virginia Tech, 37–38

Ward, Charlie, 5–7, 10

Weinke, Chris, 36–38

Williamson, Ed (coach), 13, 14

Woodham, Wally, 28

ABOUT THE AUTHOR

Alex Monnig is a freelance journalist from St. Louis, Missouri. He graduated with his master's degree from the University of Missouri in May 2010. During his career he has spent time covering sporting events around the world, including the 2008 Olympic Games in China, the 2010 Commonwealth Games in India, and the 2011 Rugby World Cup in New Zealand.